Architecture for Kids

Architecture
for Kids

AGES 8–12

Skill-Building Activities
for Future Architects

BY MARK MORENO AND SIENA MORENO

ILLUSTRATIONS BY BRUCE RANKIN

ROCKRIDGE
PRESS

Interior and Cover Designer: Erik Jacobsen
Art Producer: Samantha Ulban
Editor: Lauren Moore and Alyson Penn
Production Manager: Jose Olivera
Production Editor: Melissa Edeburn
Illustrations © 2020 Bruce Rankin. All other images used under license from Shutterstock.

ISBN: Print 978-1-64876-002-0 | eBook 978-1-64739-571-1
R0

To Tony and Pat Moreno, without whose loving
support, and gift of a student trip to Italy
36 years ago, this book would be unlikely.

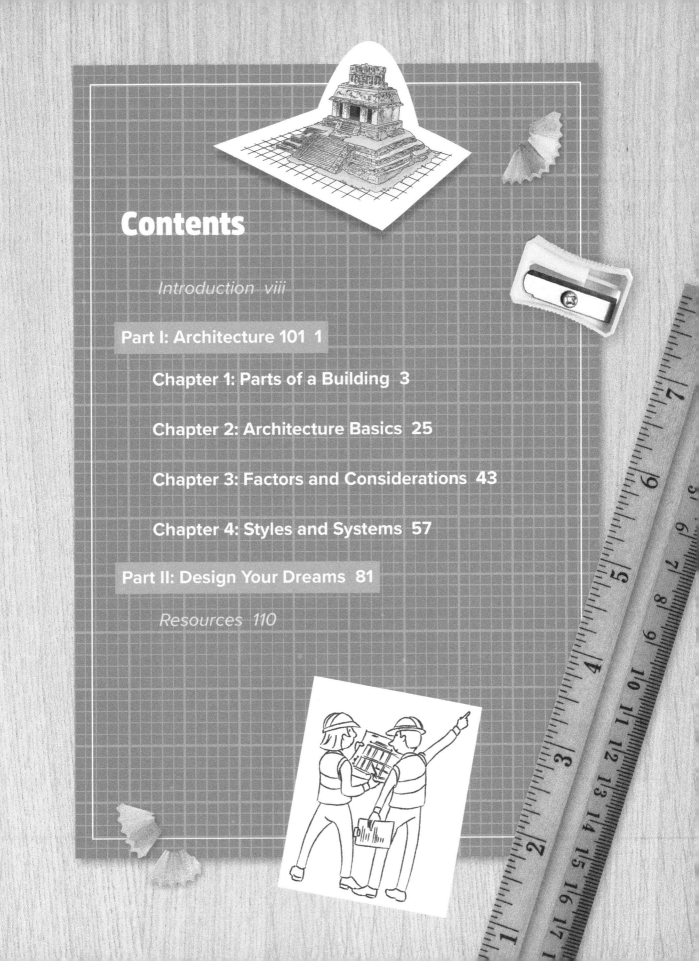

Contents

Introduction

Standing in line on college registration day, without a real clue about what I wanted to do with my life, I arbitrarily decided to study architecture because it was early in the alphabet. Within the first semester, I was hooked by the studio environment full of intellectual discourse and camaraderie with friends, and I was engrossed in the creative, hands-on learning. The potential of architecture to positively impact people's lives excited me. Now that I am a professor of architecture, and founder and director of Renaissance Kids Architecture Camp, I am privileged to share the joys of such a powerful profession.

My daughter, Siena, grew up in a family and community rich with art, creativity, and deep discussions of how our environment shapes much of what we do. Because of her love for art, architecture, and the immense power of words, Siena studied art and English in college. She is pursuing a career working with kids and adolescents because she strongly believes that incredible young minds like yours will change the world. She and I share a passion for education, making things, and having fun.

No matter who you are, this discipline has something to offer. How could it not? We are surrounded by architecture like we are surrounded by air. With your creative minds, we can always strive to make the world a better place.

ALL ABOUT ARCHITECTS

Like buildings, architects come in many types. Some are dreamers who imagine what seems impossible. Some are practical, designing for efficiency, sturdiness, and affordability. Some are a mix of both. But they all like to think of themselves as problem solvers in disciplines such as architecture, interior design, urban planning, and landscape design.

An architect is a person who designs buildings. Think about your house: the way the front looks, where the doors and windows are, and what they look like. Think about the locations of the rooms. Someone designed all that! An architect likely designed your school, your doctor's office, the mall, and every other major building in your town, too.

Architects have to consider a lot of things when they design a building. What kind of building is it? Who will be using it? What other buildings are nearby?

Remember, architecture is not just about buildings—it's also about people and how they live, work, play, worship, and so much more!

HOW TO USE THIS BOOK

This book will introduce you to key terminology and skills of building design. You'll see many examples of architectural styles from around the world and throughout history. Each new concept will be followed by an activity to help you develop creative designs, practice architectural techniques, and explore new ideas. Treat this book like a sketchbook—write in it, draw in it, brainstorm, and sketch your thoughts. At the end, you'll have a book full of your own designs: your very first portfolio!

WHAT YOU'LL NEED

The only item you really need to complete this book is a pencil or a pen. Some activities suggest other materials, such as a ruler or a deck of cards, but you'll always need some form of writing utensil. If you don't have the suggested material for an activity, get creative. Can't find a ruler or a tape measure to measure distances? Use your feet or the length of your pinky finger. Don't have ice pop sticks? Use spaghetti. Always feel free to add color to your drawings with markers, pens, colored pencils, paint, or crayons. Remember, this is *your* book! You can change the rules.

DRAWING TIPS

Drawing should be enjoyable, so sit comfortably, hold your pen or pencil lightly, and don't be afraid to change the angle of your paper. You can make lines thinner by holding your pencil upright, and thicker by angling it downward. Be gentle with yourself—nobody's drawing is perfect on the first try. Draw your first lines lightly and loosely, and then, as your drawing starts to take shape, you can make your best lines darker and bolder. Avoid erasing! Your process is just as important as your product. If you think you've made a mistake, draw over it, or draw darker to get your idea across.

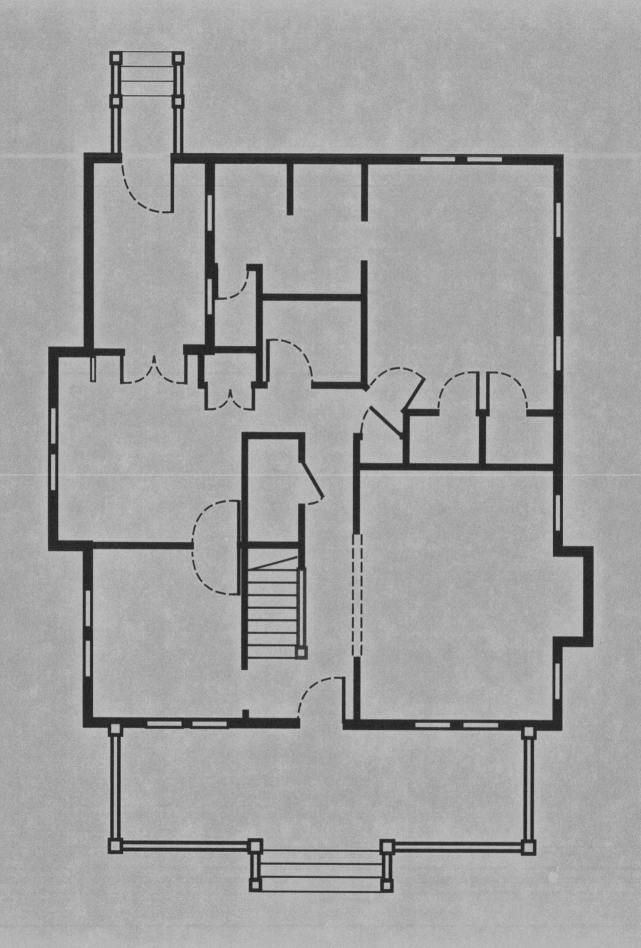

PART I

Architecture 101

CHAPTER 1

Parts of a Building

Designing buildings is a huge part of architecture, and to build a structure, an architect has to design each of the parts that make up that structure. Marcus Vitruvius was an architect who lived 2,000 years ago in ancient Rome, and he said that good architecture must be firm, useful, and delightful. This is still true today! All the parts that make up a building need to fit together physically, materially, and visually in order to create a practical, strong, beautiful structure.

This chapter will give some key information about some of the most important parts of buildings. Although every building has basic elements, such as doors and walls, one of the best things about architecture is that the architect gets to choose how things fit together, what they look like, and where they go. You're the architect in this book, so you're in charge! Let's explore some major parts of a building and see what cool designs you can come up with.

FOUNDATION

Foundations in life help us establish stability. Societies, organizations, families, and individuals depend on foundational ideas such as laws and morals.

A building's foundation, however, is physical. It's what connects a building to the ground and holds it in place. The foundation also helps distribute weight over a large area to avoid overloading the underlying earth. It also anchors the building against forces produced by wind, storms, flooding, tornadoes, or even earthquakes.

Architects design foundations to suit the conditions of their **clients'** properties, or **sites**. Some foundations lie on the ground and are called **floating slabs**. They function sort of like boats on water. For soils such as clay and sand, which are less stable, a floating slab may make the most sense. Because a floating slab is so strong and rigid, it allows the building to settle and shift as a single object and not fall apart if the ground moves unevenly. If the ground is soft or on a slope, the building may need **concrete piers** to reach deeply and find support on **bedrock** or beneath **frost lines**.

BEDROCK: hard rock beneath, or exposed at, the earth's surface—the sturdiest condition used for a building's foundation

CLIENT: the person or group for whom the architect is creating the design

CONCRETE PIERS: columnlike supports that are usually embedded into the ground to support a building's foundation

FLOATING SLABS: concrete constructs (floors) that lie over the ground, without any kind of anchoring deep into the earth; often used in residential and light industrial buildings

FROST LINE: The depth below ground where a piece of land typically stays unfrozen all winter

SITE: an area of ground where a structure or structures can be built

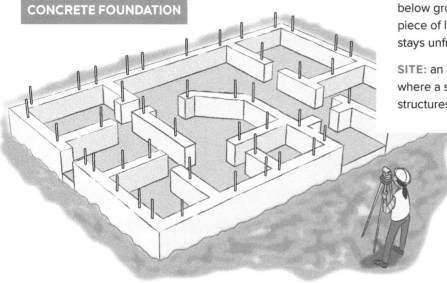

CONCRETE FOUNDATION

SHAKY FOUNDATION

With this activity, you'll explore how foundations affect the way structures can be built. For this activity, you'll need:

- One cake pan that fits flat in the kitchen sink
- Index cards (any size)

Steps:

1. Use the cake pan as the foundation to build a structure of cards.

2. Build the house as tall as you can, and measure its height.

3. Draw your creation here, but imagine it's a real building in a real landscape. Try to emphasize the most basic shapes that are foundational to architectural form—rectangles!

4. Dismantle the structure (okay, blow it down—it's more fun this way!).

5. Do the exercise again, but this time, place the cake pan in enough water that it floats freely. Then build a structure as tall as before.

6. Draw the building again, but think about its new context in water. How does this affect the way you imagine the structure?

STRUCTURE

Architects often refer to a building's structural frame as its skeleton. The frame is what provides support to the building, and the outer walls enclose the space. Sometimes load-bearing walls do both! These components need to be made out of strong materials such as wood, concrete, brick, or metal.

Architects hire engineers to make sure the structure can hold the weight of the building itself, which is referred to as **dead load**. Architects also need to consider the weight of **live load**—for example, furniture and people inside the building, and snow and wind, which put pressure on the outside. All the materials that make up a building's construction generally support one another in two ways: **compression** (such as bricks stacked in a masonry wall) or **tension** (for example, steel cable bracing that keeps a frame rigid).

COMPRESSION: characteristic of a building block or structure that withstands pressure—examples are bricks, stones, and blocks

DEAD LOAD: the total weight of a building's structural or permanent elements such as walls, beams, ceilings, roofs, and air conditioning systems

LIVE LOAD: the total weight of non-permanent or temporary elements in or on a building, such as snow, rain, people, furniture, and aardvarks

TENSION: characteristic of a building or structure that withstands stretching and bending forces—for example, steel, rebar, and cables

STEEL FRAME

BUILDING FRIENDSHIPS

This activity is all about relationships and support.

Draw two or more structures that incorporate the idea of friendship. Sketch out different design ideas for ways to add support or balance. Now try building them from household elements. Use whatever you have handy in the house—cardboard boxes, Legos, ice pop sticks, tape, pasta, hot glue, toothpicks, string, stuff like that. Then draw what you've built to compare before and after sketches.

Remember, your sketches and initial ideas don't have to be perfect. Sketchbooks are meant for brainstorming, practicing, and developing. They can have a mix of drawings and notes, and they can overlap and be messy.

WALLS

A building's walls enclose and protect the interior and the people inside.

An architect has to think about two kinds of walls when designing a building: exterior walls and interior walls. Exterior walls have to be strong and weather-resistant on the outside, and they can be made of stone, brick, concrete, wood, or even glass. A building's interior walls separate its rooms and provide privacy. Interior walls are often constructed with wooden or metal **studs** and **drywall**.

Architects have to consider the physical impact of walls, such as the type of **insulation** they provide and the kind of weather conditions they can withstand. But an architect needs to remember that walls can have a social and emotional impact as well. A small **enclosure** that doesn't get much light can provide a sense of comfort and safety, but it could also make people feel confined (closed in) or even claustrophobic.

DRYWALL: a type of panel made from plaster or fibrous products and usually screwed to studs to form the interior walls of buildings

ENCLOSURE: an area surrounded by walls

FOUNDATION WALL: a wall built into the ground to support the structure above it

GARDEN WALL: a wall in or around a garden

INSULATION: material typically used in walls, under roofs, and above ceilings to impede the transfer of heat or sound from one place to another

RETAINING WALL: a wall designed and built to withstand the forces of earth on one side

STUD: a support in a framed wall that drywall or other surfaces are attached to

STONE **CLAY BRICK**

WOOD **CONCRETE**

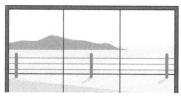

GLASS

SKETCHING WALLS

Walk around your neighborhood and find as many types of walls as you can. Draw them here. You can include fences, screens, **retaining walls**, **foundation walls**, and **garden walls**.

Write notes on your drawings to identify the materials used to build the walls and how they fit or do not fit with their surroundings. Some architects design their walls to look like they've always been there; others try to make their walls (and buildings) stand out. Do you see some that seem to stand out, and others that fit into their surroundings? Compare and contrast the walls you find.

DOORS

Doors allow people living in or visiting a building to come and go easily. Doors are part of a building's walls, but they're not part of the structure. They have a frame made of **jambs**, **headers**, and **thresholds**, and most doors are supported by hinges so they can swing freely. But doors aren't just functional—in fact, they can contribute a great deal to a building's attitude. Doors communicate characteristics, such as strength, formality, inclusion, and peacefulness. Large, ornate doors, such as those on churches and courthouses, encourage visitors to enter quietly and respectfully. A brightly painted door on a quaint cottage, on the other hand, conveys a more casual greeting.

In addition, the design of a door can either exclude people or invite connection. For instance, locked or narrow doors can create a frustrating situation for people in wheelchairs, but wide-open archways and doors with large windows encourage everyone to pass through.

HEADER: the beam-like piece that spans over a door or window and supports weight from elements above

JAMBS: the vertical sides of a door's frame; swinging doors usually have a hinge side and a latch side

THRESHOLD: the material that forms the bottom of a doorway; this term is also used to describe the idea of passage or transition more generally

DIFFERENT TYPES OF DOORS

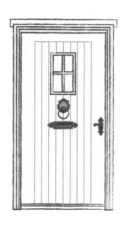

CASTLE VS. COTTAGE

A castle would have a pretty different door than a cottage. First, draw the kind of door that comes to mind as you're designing a castle. Then draw the kind of door you would use for a cottage. What are the main differences between the two?

Door for castle:

Material: _____   Shape: _____   Size: _____

Door for cottage:

Material: _____   Shape: _____   Size: _____

WINDOWS

Where doors provide physical access to places, windows provide visual access to the world outside. Like doors, windows are both functional and a design element. They let air, light, and sound into and out of buildings, and they come in all shapes and sizes.

You can choose from many window types for all sorts of conditions. Awning windows swing out and protect from rain with hinges at the top of their **sashes**. Double-hung windows slide up and down to allow cool air to reach low spots and warm air to escape from high spots. Casement windows can catch and direct glancing breezes for greater interior comfort.

Special types of windows—such as bay windows, picture windows, and clerestory windows—add value to people's experiences in a space. Bay windows often provide a place for someone to sit while enjoying a panoramic view. Picture windows are large and give a wide view of the landscape. Clerestory windows let in light from above, often just below the ceiling, while maintaining privacy.

SASH: a frame that holds each piece of glass in a window

SLIDING GLASS DOORS

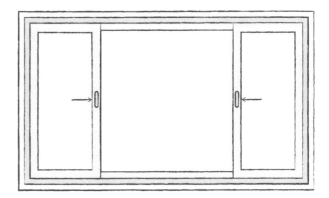

BAY WINDOW

WORLD WITHOUT WINDOWS

What would the world be like without windows? Draw a picture of a few of the houses or buildings on your street, but without windows.

How do these windowless buildings make you feel?

_____

Do they encourage a sense of community, or do they feel unwelcoming?

_____

How would you feel if your house had no windows?

_____

ROOF

A building without a roof would be weird, right? A roof protects a building's interior and the people inside. It must be able to shed water, keep the weather elements outside, and help control inside air temperature.

Roofs can add character to buildings and even the surrounding community. In fact, some of the most recognizable buildings in the world, such as the Pantheon, the Sydney Opera House, the Milwaukee Art Museum, the Taj Mahal, and Saint Basil's Cathedral, are famous because of their roofs.

If designed well, a roof can foreshadow and build anticipation for the experience of entering and moving through a building. A roofed porch can help make a soft transition indoors from the outside, and it especially increases the time—both during the day and throughout the year—that people can stay outdoors, connecting to nature and the neighborhood.

Roofs covered with plants, called green roofs, are increasingly popular to manage water **runoff** and combat climate change. Some roofs feature decks and gardens so that people can occupy these spaces, giving buildings a whole new level of purpose and enjoyment.

RUNOFF: when more water—rain or snow—lands on a building or site than it can absorb

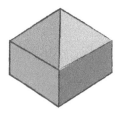

PYRAMID ROOF

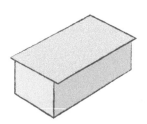

FLAT ROOF

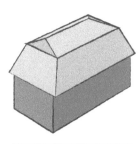

MANSARD ROOF

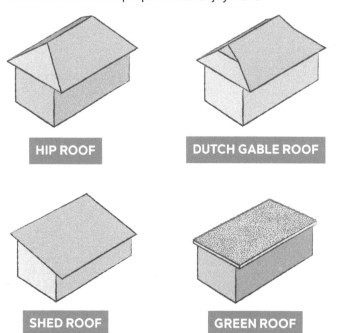

HIP ROOF

DUTCH GABLE ROOF

SHED ROOF

GREEN ROOF

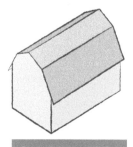

GAMBREL ROOF

A ROOF OVER YOUR HEAD

Pictured here are some buildings with roofs that may not make them famous but are unique and recognizable as being handmade, authentic, homelike, and associated with a particular country or people. Structures and roofs like these are often built by people in the community, not by those we think of today as professional tradespeople.

These Turkish buildings' roof shape and materials are time-tested and well-suited to their desert environment. The roof height and shape mean that hot air rises, and cool air is circulated below. By day, the thick mud-brick walls trap the sun's heat, which radiates inward to keep the interior relatively warm in the evening, when the temperature drops.

On the basis of the climate and natural materials where you live, draw a plan for a roof. Does your area get a lot of heavy snow, or is it sunny and dry? What sort of nearby plants, trees or other materials could you use to make a roof?

BEEHIVE-DOMED HOUSES IN HARRAN, TURKEY

FLOOR

Buildings' floors help contain spaces, but they're different from walls and roofs because they separate us from the earth below. Floors are like interior landscapes and must be strong enough to support furniture and hold up to people walking on them every day. Architects often use varying floor materials for different uses. For instance, a kitchen or bathroom floor may have ceramic tile, concrete, or waterproof vinyl to withstand spills. Living rooms and dining rooms may have natural wood or bamboo flooring to seem warmer and cozier. Bedroom floors are often covered with carpeting for more comfort when you're rolling out of bed barefoot.

Floors are easiest to walk on when they're flat, but architects can bend or fold the floor into ramps and stairs to go up or down. Architecture is increasingly designed to accommodate those who need wheelchairs or rolling walkers to get around, such as people with physical disabilities and older adults. More buildings today have flatter floors and include ramps and elevators.

FLOORS IN A HOUSE

STEPPING OUTSIDE

Pick a room in your home that is next to an outdoor space. Design an outdoor patio and pavilion that is adjacent to (next to) that room. Think about ease of access, natural flow of circulation (people moving around), and how the inside floor and outside floors work together. Draw your design here.

Room: _____

Space outside the room: _____

How I will make them work together:_____

Design:

STAIRS, ELEVATORS, AND RAMPS

When a building has more than one level, there must be a way for people to move from floor to floor. As mentioned in the last section, this is accomplished with stairs, ramps, and elevators. These all provide **vertical circulation**, but there is no one-size-fits-all approach to every building. Stairs are not usable for people in wheelchairs and strollers. Ramps can be long or slippery. And elevators work well, until there's a power outage or a fire. Trying to escape a burning building by using the elevator would be like trying to get out through a smoke-filled chimney.

All buildings must meet **code** requirements, meaning that they are safe and accessible for everyone. To achieve this, architects must often include a combination of stairs, elevators, and ramps in their designs to accommodate **occupants** with different abilities.

Many architects choose to embrace this necessity and design these elements as celebrated architectural features. However, we don't have perfect solutions yet. Can you help think of some?

CODE: a set of agreed-on rules for a city, state, or country that specifies the standards (especially for safety) for constructing buildings and other structures

OCCUPANT: the person or group of people who live in or use a building

VERTICAL CIRCULATION: the ways that occupants in a building or landscape move between floors and different levels—typically stairs, ramps, and elevators

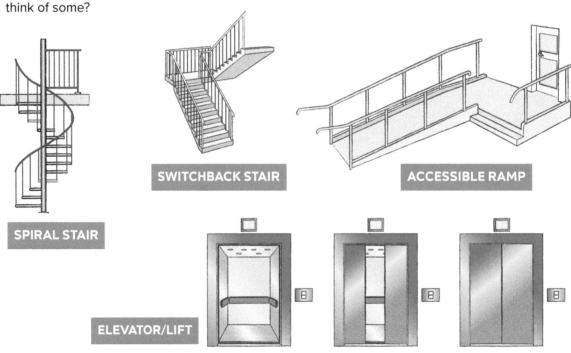

SWITCHBACK STAIR

ACCESSIBLE RAMP

SPIRAL STAIR

ELEVATOR/LIFT

AN UPHILL BATTLE

In Greek mythology, King Sisyphus was destined by fate to roll a large rock up a hill, only to have it roll down every time before it reached the top. In the space here, draw a comic strip showing Sisyphus using stairs, ramps, elevators, or any combination of these to transport the rock to the hilltop.

Keep in mind that all new approaches to solving problems can fail—many times. It's up to you to decide whether Sisyphus finally wins. Also consider any other devices he might need, because according to the myth, that rock was really big!

FINISHES AND ORNAMENTATION

Remember Marcus Vitruvius from the introduction to this chapter? He wanted to make sure that buildings were not just useful and sturdy but also delightful! There are lots of ways to add delightfulness to a building. One way is to incorporate intricate and beautiful characteristics into functional things. Some examples are column **capitals**, which carry loads to columns, and stone gargoyles, which carry water off roofs and away from buildings. Another way is to apply nonfunctional ornamentation, for example, a small decorative gingerbread trim on a Victorian house or a colorful wreath on a door. Parts of a building can be designed to look functional but are actually just decorative. Examples include window shutters and roof brackets.

Some styles of architecture and design don't involve much ornamentation at all, whereas others use a lot of it. You'll learn more about some of the different architecture and design styles in chapter 4.

CAPITAL: the topmost part of a classical column, often decorated according to the rules of the classical orders—Doric, Ionic, and Corinthian

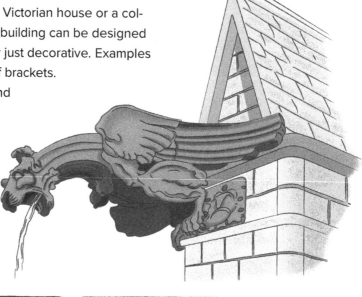

GARGOYLE

DORIC CAPITAL   IONIC CAPITAL   CORINTHIAN CAPITAL

FINISH THE COLUMNS

The columns pictured here don't quite reach the roof. Can you help? Design your own column capitals on this building. The design for classical Corinthian capitals was based on acanthus leaves. What will you use for inspiration? Butterfly wings? Maybe bird feathers? Anything goes—remember, you're the architect! In addition to fixing the missing capitals, what else can you do to add ornamentation to this building?

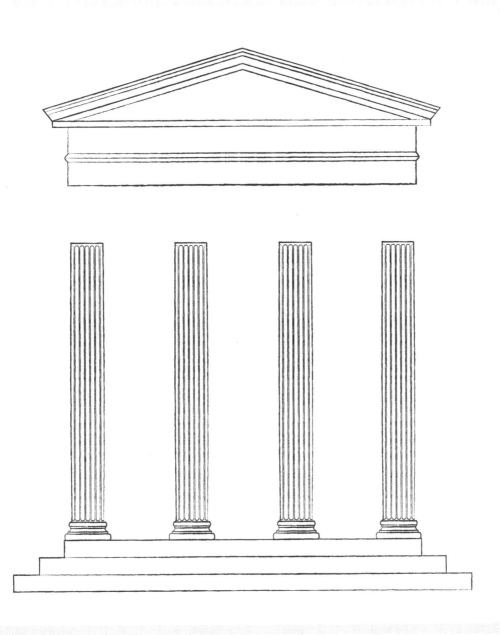

CHAPTER CHALLENGE

In these pages, design a fort for your bedroom. Remember to think about what you learned in this chapter. Carefully consider the materials and construction methods you would use to create the foundation, structure, floors, walls, roof, doorways, windows, and ornamentation. Maybe you can build a second level with stairs or a ramp. Try to make your construction firm, useful, and delightful on both the inside and the outside. Can components have more than one purpose? Could a window provide light and have a shelf to store things? Could a wall serve as part of your structure and also be decorative? Get creative! Now see if you can actually build a model of the fort in your bedroom out of materials you have in your house.

Sketching tip: Architects often do many drawings for one building. Feel free to make a large drawing of the whole fort, along with a few smaller drawings to emphasize cool details. Architects also draw the same feature in a couple of ways to see which version they like best. You have plenty of space here, so don't be afraid to use it!

CHAPTER 2

Architecture Basics

Architects serve an important role in helping people, buildings, and cities thrive. They oversee and coordinate the efforts of many people in different professions, including engineering, landscape design, and interior design. Architects like to solve complex problems, and their unique training prepares them to face challenges by understanding the full context (or big picture) and focusing on details. For architects and designers, the best tools are their ideas and drawings. In this chapter, we'll explore important ideas and necessary drawing types related to making places. Pay attention to how architects position themselves to see things from different vantage points: from high above, from the side, and from the inside, as well as three-dimensionally.

SITE PLAN

A site plan is a drawing from a **bird's-eye view** that represents a property's size and shape. It includes anything that is attached to the ground: buildings, trees, sidewalks, and even mailboxes. To build in an earth-friendly way, the site plan would make sure that all new **building footprints** respect the property's natural setting and **habitat** as much as possible. A site plan illustrates the types of buildings on the site and how they relate to the land and neighboring sites. It shows how water and pedestrians circulate or flow throughout the site, and how cars and utilities (such as electricity and gas) get to the site. A site plan also helps an architect secure a building permit, which allows the structure to be built.

BIRD'S-EYE VIEW: the view from a vantage point above what is being looked at

BUILDING FOOT-PRINTS: the perimeter and space inside any part of a building that touches the ground

HABITAT: a kind of natural environment where a particular species of organism lives

NORTH ARROW: a drawn arrow that represents which way is north on a plan view. From this diagram, you can figure out which way is east, south, and west.

ROOF PLAN: a view of a roof as if looking straight down at it from above

SITE PLAN

- Shed
- Vegetables
- Porch
- Greenhouse
- Rock garden
- Tiles
- Path
- Garden bed
- Pond and wet area
- Garden beds
- Parking
- N

BIRD'S-EYE VIEW

Draw the footprint, or **roof plan**, of your home and its property on the graph paper here. This is a bird's-eye view of the structure where you live and its surroundings. Include anything that's attached to the soil, such as trees, sidewalks, and lampposts. To provide more context, you can add neighboring properties and a **north arrow**.

For extra fun, consider designing changes for your property. You might want to add a swimming pool or a swing set—or maybe go all-out and add your own tennis or basketball court.

Sketching tip: Don't worry about measuring and drawing everything perfectly. This drawing is more about seeing the big picture than focusing on exact details.

SECTION

When engineers want to understand machines, they take them apart. When scientists want to view the inside of a frog or other animal, they dissect it. To show how a building space works or how a wall or roof is made, architects draw a section. Imagine a dollhouse that has been cut in half down the middle. A sheet of glass is placed against the whole side of one half of the dollhouse where it was cut. That sheet of glass is a good representation of your cutting plane because it touches all the parts of the dollhouse that became exposed when the dollhouse was cut down the middle. Now imagine tracing with a washable marker only the parts of the dollhouse that touch the glass. This type of drawing is called a *section drawing*.

A section helps architects make structural frames more efficient and spatially pleasing. It also helps them figure out the angle of the sun at specific times and during different seasons. This allows architects to consider and control temperatures, see how spaces interact with nature, and plan for views. A section drawing can also help determine the best roof angle to catch sun rays if solar panels will be added.

INTERIOR ELEVATION: the wall farthest from the viewer in a section drawing. The interior elevation can include windows, doors, furniture, and decorations, but everything is shown as orthogonal, meaning not showing perspective.

DOLL HOUSE SECTION

CUT IN HALF

Sit in your favorite space in your house, and look around to decide where your cutting plane will be. For example, if your favorite space is your bedroom, imagine cutting the room in half with an imaginary saw. Anything that was cut by the saw would touch the cutting plane. Create a section drawing of what you see. Be sure to include the back wall farthest from you, called the **interior elevation**, and add any windows, doors, and furnishings (furniture and decor) that are visible beyond the cutting plane. This is kind of like drawing what you see inside a dollhouse.

Now imagine that someone has asked you to modify the space. They would like this space to be twice as tall and to include stairs that lead to a second level that overlooks the first. Or think about how you could change the space in response to a new fad.

ELEVATION/FACADE

Our faces are one of the most important ways we express our moods and feelings. A building's face, called an elevation or facade, works the same way. People can change their facial expressions in an instant, but a building's expression is harder to adjust. For that reason, it's important for architects to understand the intended public message for the building they're designing. Doors and windows are sometimes referred to as a building's eyes because they greatly affect mood. Roof heights, overhangs, porches, and stairs do, too.

As an architect, you'll want to consider what the building type says to the public. If you're designing a bank, you want the facade to say "safe and secure." If you're designing a library, the facade should say "quiet and peaceful." What's great about architecture in all cultures is its creative and infinite ability to be expressive, just like the human face!

ELEVATION OF A HOUSE

AWESOME ANALYTIQUE

An *analytique* is a type of drawing that collages different parts of a facade together (a collage is a collection of images arranged on a surface). It generally includes a drawing of the full elevation, which is a small component of the composition. Smaller, decorative parts of the facade, such as a column capital or a beautiful light fixture, are often made into a larger part of the overall drawing.

   Create an analytique of one of your favorite nearby buildings—maybe it's a library, city hall, a museum, or a beautiful church. Use separate pieces of paper to make rough sketches of the individual components so you can move them around to play with the composition. Once you're happy with your arrangement, redraw the components as one piece on this page.

ANALYTIQUE

SCALE AND PROPORTION

If architects designed buildings at their actual size, their paper would need to be bigger than the buildings! Instead, they use the idea of *scale* to represent the sizes of things. A site plan may easily show a property at a scale of 1 inch on paper equals 20 feet, or even 100 feet, in person. A typical drawing of a house floor plan is often scaled down to ¼ inch equals 1 foot. A tool called an *architect's scale* helps designers more easily draw at different scales.

Proportion is a bit different; it is generally about comparing the sizes of two or more things. Think of a building that's twice the height of another. If a building's height is three times its width, then its height-to-width proportion is described as the ratio 3 to 1. Buildings with a width-to-height ratio of 4 to 1 (or 8 to 1!) would be wider than they are tall.

ELEVATION SITE PLAN

1 INCH = 20 FEET

THE GOLDEN RECTANGLE

Art and architectural history suggest there is an ideal rectangle with a ratio of about 1 to 1.618. This is often referred to as the *golden rectangle*. This ratio has mystified people for hundreds of years because it seems random, and yet it shows up in many natural elements! It exists in plants, flowers, snail shells, pine cones, and seed patterns.

Artists and architects have used the ratio of the golden rectangle to help guide their designs for more than 1,000 years, and it continues to be used today. The illustration that follows shows you how to make your own golden rectangle. Grab a piece of paper and draw a large golden rectangle, and then draw a building facade inside it. For an added challenge, draw smaller golden rectangles to create components of your facade. Maybe they will become windows, towers, or a porch.

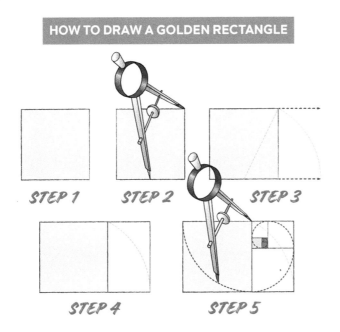

HOW TO DRAW A GOLDEN RECTANGLE

STEP 1

STEP 2

STEP 3

STEP 4

STEP 5

STEP 1
Draw a square

STEP 2
Place the compass point at the halfway mark of the bottom line

STEP 3
Draw an arc from the top right hand corner to the bottom

STEP 4
Draw a rectangle next to the square

STEP 5
Draw smaller squares in each rectangle that is formed and make an arc in each one to complete the spiral then draw the arc in the first large square

FLOOR PLAN

Remember our discussion about a section being an imaginary vertical cut through a building? Well, if you turn the cutting plane horizontally and remove the upper building portion to look down, you're looking at a floor plan. Drawings of a floor plan help people see how rooms connect and how an entire level of a building might look. Floor plans can be simple or so detailed with furnishings that they become art. If an architect is creating a simple, practical building, they might produce a clean, basic floor plan. However, if they are designing a more artistic, creative building, they will often want to draw more attractive and full floor plans.

DIMENSIONS: the measurements of all sides and features of an object

FLOOR PLAN OF A HOUSE

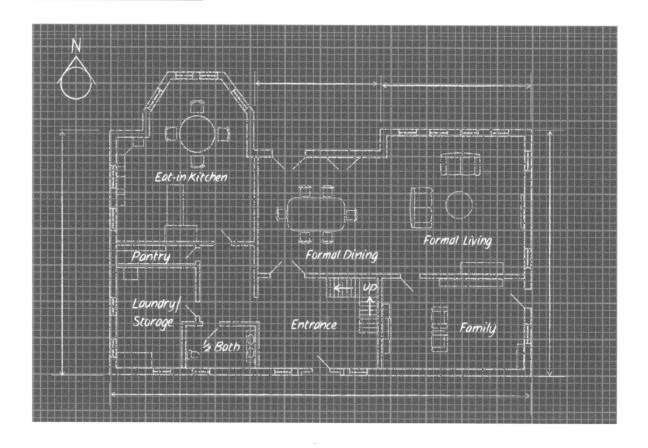

DRAWING FLOOR PLANS

Draw the floor plan of at least three rooms in a building where you spend a lot of time. This can be your school, your best friend's house, a community center, or even your own home—whatever you like! Choose rooms that connect to each other so you can see how they interact in your floor plan. Also measure the walls, doors, windows, and furnishings. Transfer the **dimensions** of these elements to the graph paper one at a time. This is a great chance to design all-new furniture for these rooms. You may want to draw the pieces of furniture on separate sheets of paper so you can cut them out and rearrange them on your floor plan here.

   Think about the concepts from the earlier section about scale and proportion, and scale down your measurements to fit on the page.

FUNCTION

The purpose and form of a space come primarily from its function, or how it will be used. How people use a space might be the most important thing to consider when designing a building. Different functions call for different materials, layouts, flow patterns, lighting, finishes, and more.

Some spaces in a building have more than one function. Kitchens, for instance, have become a place not only to prepare food but also to hang out with friends and family. And many bedrooms don't just have beds—they have desks, toys, and TVs that fit into how the occupant wants to use the space. Many families also integrate technology into their homes to use spaces more safely, comfortably, and conveniently.

A PLACE FOR FAMILY LIFE

A PLACE FOR STUDYING AND SOCIALIZING

OUT OF THIS WORLD

Chicago architect Louis Sullivan said that "form follows function." He meant that architects design spaces based on how people of that time want to use those spaces. Imagine you're an architect for an extraterrestrial society that lives totally differently than humans do. Design a house for one out-of-this-world family. What if their gravity is reversed so everything has to be tied down? Do they have a garage for their spaceships, or do they park them on the roof?

Name of extraterrestrial family: _____

My extraterrestrial family lives on the planet _____.

My extraterrestrial family's house looks like:

3D DRAWINGS

Imagine driving down a long, straight road. The houses right next to you look normal size, but the buildings two blocks away look really small, right? They look tiny because of our **perspective**. With three-dimensional (3D) drawings, we make some things appear to be really close to the viewer, and some far away.

With 2D drawings, such as site plans and floor plans, we see the length and width but not the height of objects. With elevation and section drawings, we see the width and height but not the depth of objects. In these 2D drawing types, we can only see two dimensions at a time. However, in 3D drawings, such as a **plan oblique**, architects can show more of a structure's full form. In another type of 3D drawing, called a *perspective drawing*, they can show what our eyes actually see.

PARALLEL: lines that extend in the same direction and never intersect

PERSPECTIVE: Mostly in drawings and paintings, perspective offers a realistic 3D feeling to a flat or 2D image. It gives the illusion of accuracy and depth; objects appear smaller and closer together in the artist's distant view.

PLAN OBLIQUE: A measurable drawing that does not diminish the size of distant objects, as perspective drawings do. It begins with a floor plan rotated usually to 30, 45, or 60 degrees on the page, and then the corners are projected straight up to depict heights.

VANISHING POINT: in a perspective drawing, the point in front of the viewer, generally at eye level; parallel lines in reality converge (vanish) here at an imaginary horizon line

THREE-POINT PERSPECTIVE DRAWING

FINISH THE SCENE

In this lightened perspective drawing, you can see that some buildings and their character are missing from the streetscape. Your client would like you to finish the drawing by following the rules of a one-point perspective. Lines that are parallel in reality, like the curb, tops of doors and flat roofs, all aim at the vanishing point at the end of the street.

You can also decorate and modify any existing buildings to make the street a more pleasant place to be. Use your imagination!

Sketching tip: Perspective drawings can be difficult, so just do your best. You can always use a ruler and lightly draw all your horizontal lines extra long so they end at the vanishing point. This will help you make sure all your lines are angled correctly.

CHAPTER CHALLENGE

This chapter challenge involves two different spaces. Design an architecture makerspace—a collaborative workspace for making, learning, exploring, and sharing technology, tools, and especially ideas—that's just for kids. It should be a place where kids can enter through a large brick archway to work together on architecture projects. In an adjacent space connected by another brick archway, design a smoothie shop where kids can socialize and hold meetings in small or medium-sized groups.

First, represent your designs with an architectural program—this is a written description of a client's needs, wants, and dreams for a building—to explain your general idea. Then draw a floor plan, an exterior elevation, a section, and a 3D view to show the various parts and vantage points of your design.

For both places, make sure you think about the needs for each business, including *front-of-house* functions and *back-of-house* spaces. Front-of-house elements are any spaces, objects, or services that a customer can see and access, such as tables and chairs for gathering and working, the counter where you can order a smoothie, and public restrooms. Back-of-house spaces are places that only employees can go, such as the kitchen, storage area, or office.

CHAPTER 3

Factors and Considerations

A rchitects need to examine countless factors and considerations when designing a building. To do this, architects generally follow a design process that helps them explore questions along the way. First comes the idea phase of design, called *schematic design*, which focuses on general issues and questions. What type of building does the client want? Who will live, play, or work there? Approximately where will the building site be? How will the building relate to its immediate surroundings?

The *design development* phase comes next. This is when the architect figures out the specifics. Where exactly on the site will the structure be? How will it be oriented—will the building face north, south, east, or west? How will the spaces function? What materials will be used for construction?

Next, the architect draws up a legal set of *construction documents*. These are the instructions that the builders will use when they are actually building the structure. These documents include site plans, floor plans, elevations, sections, and other very detailed drawings. Along with these drawings comes a written document, called the *specifications*, that explains what materials to use and how to install them.

BUILDING TYPE

A building's type most closely relates to how it will typically be used. For instance, a museum is a building type. But we can also get more specific, like a history museum, an art museum, or a children's museum. How might those differ from one another?

Building types can also be referred to by their different characteristics. For example, a skyscraper is a building type with a focus on size. Heavy timber, steel-framed, or masonry buildings are good examples of building types that relate to their materials or construction methods.

In places where buildings are closely gathered, such as traditional towns and bigger cities, urban designers and architects refer to *background*-type buildings; these are typically basic in appearance and are more common in our daily lives, such as homes and shops. *Foreground* buildings stand out more based on their appearance, and they have a more communal or civic or religious purpose; examples are public libraries, state capitols, and houses of worship.

The design process can be very different depending on the building type. For example, a house only has to meet the needs of one family, but skyscrapers and hospitals must satisfy the needs of thousands of people every day. The larger and more technical a building is, the more complex it is to design, build, operate, and maintain.

BUILDING TYPES IN A CITY

IF MY FAMILY WAS A CITY . . .

On a separate piece of paper, draw each of your friends or family members without drawing a person—draw only buildings, structures, and objects. For example, if I drew my mother as a building, she would be a puzzle factory. She loves to put together jigsaw puzzles, and when I was a kid, puzzles were one of the most special activities we did together.

Next, cut out each building and assemble them side by side on the street here. Think about whether each should be a foreground or background building, and arrange them accordingly. For fun, add other items as appropriate for each building, such as trees, sidewalks, lampposts, and benches.

IMMEDIATE SURROUNDINGS

Architects use **site analyses** and **land surveys** when they consider how buildings will work with or against their immediate surroundings. They will determine whether the soil, site, and region are suitable for building. This is partly for the owner's sake, but also to protect each region's unique characteristics and natural ecosystem.

Clients often want shops and services conveniently located and close by. A family might want a school or park within walking distance of their home. Workers in an office building would like restaurants close enough for lunch breaks. Architects also take potential views and nearby noise into account when they select and design for a site.

Visually, consider how a building fits in with other buildings near it. A castle in the middle of a suburban neighborhood or a log cabin in downtown Chicago might look silly.

Depending on the larger **vernacular** context—whether urban or rural, mountainous or coastal—the immediate surroundings offer countless variables for design consideration.

LAND SURVEY: a process for determining features, ponds, slopes, boundaries, and other measurements of a property. It is useful for learning how best to develop or build on a property.

SITE ANALYSIS: a predesign study conducted to understand the climate, geography, history, legalities, and infrastructural context of a specific property

VERNACULAR ARCHITECTURE: local architecture built by the local people, generally without help from high-tech tools and professionals such as architects and engineers

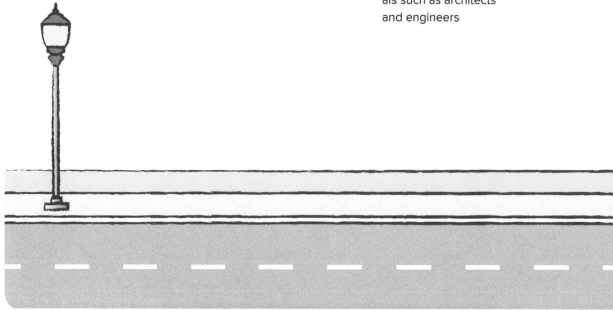

DREAM SURROUNDINGS

If you were an architect planning to build your dream home, what five things would make your immediate surroundings feel unique and special? Illustrate and label them here.

My Five Things:

1. _____
2. _____
3. _____
4. _____
5. _____

LOCATION AND ORIENTATION

Architects have to think about location when they design buildings. For example, when designing a building in a big city, architects need to consider nearby shared resources, such as sidewalks, lampposts, and sewer systems. A rural design, on the other hand, will be focused more on the natural setting. Is the landscape flat or hilly? Might the trees' root systems affect the foundations or septic system?

Regardless of location, though, buildings are continually exposed to all types of weather. Unlike people, who can move around or put on a jacket or sunhat, buildings require creative design for them to handle the weather and sun. Architects use **passive design** solutions to locate and orient their structures to manage the sun's effects on both the buildings and the people inside. For instance, architects can orient buildings close to deciduous (leafy) trees. These trees provide shade in the summer and allow sun rays to warm buildings in the winter, when the trees lose their leaves. Similarly, evergreen trees protect buildings from extremely cold winter winds.

PASSIVE DESIGN: using design techniques that take advantage of the existing climate to maintain a comfortable temperature range in the home

ARCHITECTURE CONNECTS PEOPLE WITH NATURE

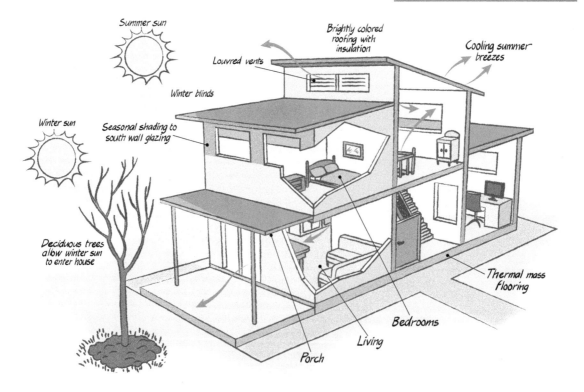

Summer sun

Brightly colored roofing with insulation

Louvred vents

Cooling summer breezes

Winter blinds

Winter sun

Seasonal shading to south wall glazing

Deciduous trees allow winter sun to enter house

Thermal mass flooring

Bedrooms

Living

Porch

CLIMATE CHANGE

Here is a footprint outline of a house. Design the floor plan and decide the best ways to respond to the site, sun, and climate. Would you rather have a bedroom window or a dining room window facing the sunrise in the east? What will be the best location, orientation, and design to help keep the house and its occupants cool in the summer and warm in the winter?

- This house will be in a cold climate with heavy winter winds from the northwest and summer winds from the southwest.

- The site has both deciduous and evergreen trees, so make sure you take into account how they will affect the building's design.

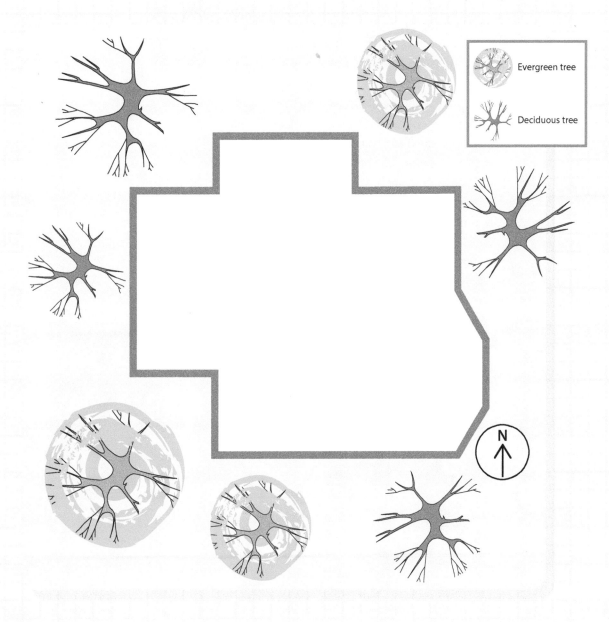

Evergreen tree

Deciduous tree

CLIMATE FACTORS

When designing buildings, it's important to consider extreme geological and climate conditions, such as earthquakes, hurricanes, and blizzards. Architects receive special training and earn licenses to design for the extreme climate factors of their location. For example, architects who are only licensed in Wisconsin cannot legally design a building for California if they haven't received training in earthquake design.

The way that buildings in some places respond to extreme conditions helps define them architecturally. Cultures in the Middle East, Africa, and the Mediterranean frequently use heavy wall masses to absorb heat by day, which then help warm inside spaces during the colder nights. People whose communities experience hurricanes and tsunamis often build structures on strong stilts to avoid destruction by high water. Tornadoes can lead to the complete destruction of anything on the ground, so the solution is often to go underground! Basements and other underground shelters are common in tornado-prone regions.

HOUSES ON STILTS IN HURRICANE ZONE

AMAZING ADVERTISEMENT

You are an expert architect! Choose an extreme climate type that your architecture firm (or office) focuses on: hurricanes, blizzards, earthquakes, or tornadoes. Design a full-page advertisement for your firm that highlights your specialty.

Name of company: _____

Extreme climate: _____

OCCUPANTS

Buildings are for people! They must be designed for the occupants' safety and overall health and wellness. Did you know that natural light, clean air, and comfortable interior spaces can help your health and productivity? Did you also know studies have shown that hospital patients often heal faster when they have access to natural views and sunlight?

To ensure safety and accessibility, cities, states, and countries create **building codes**. For instance, they make sure all people can access buildings easily. Similarly, fire codes determine how many people can safely be in a building at one time, and they guide us to make sure safe exits are available in case of an emergency.

But what about comfort? People like to have control over their personal space, so architects incorporate customizable elements into their designs. Examples are **nonfixed seating**, variable temperature and lighting controls, and different places for shade or sunshine in an outdoor space.

BUILDING CODES: a set of rules that indicate how buildings and other structures must conform to standards that protect public health, safety, and general welfare, as well as accessibility standards (an example is wheelchair access)

NONFIXED SEATING: seating in a classroom or other public venue that is flexible—meaning, the occupants can move the seats around (they are not bolted to the floor)

SPACES SERVING NEEDS

UPDATE YOUR HOME!

Design some modifications for your home based on your family members' input. Interview everyone who lives in your home. Ask them what they would change about the home. How could the kitchen serve them better? What would make the living room an even more friendly place for them? This is all about how the house serves its occupants.

   After you've interviewed everyone, design changes to your home based on their answers. Draw your designs here.

What my family wants to change about our home:

- _____
- _____
- _____
- _____

- _____
- _____
- _____

Draw your designs here:

CHAPTER CHALLENGE

Your client is a school principal who wants to build a new elementary school across town. They have already purchased the land, and they want you to design the site. The location has a couple of tricky natural elements and some interesting neighbors. How will you work with or against the surroundings to create the best possible school?

- The lot just south of the site has a gravel business. It's very noisy.

- The soil in the area is very moist, and you live in a very rainy climate. How can you design a playground that doesn't get too muddy?

- The road to the west of the site is a very busy three-lane boulevard. How will you position the school to keep students safe as they arrive and leave?

CHAPTER 4

Styles and Systems

J ust like clothing, fashion, and music, architecture goes through style trends, too. Architectural styles evolve culturally with different locations, construction methods, materials, and people's tastes and cool new ideas. Some have become so popular that they expand into different parts of the world and last for thousands of years. Vernacular styles, on the other hand, tend to reflect specific cultures and stay very close to their origins. Because buildings last for so long, architectural styles tend to change more slowly than clothing styles. However, with more efficient construction methods and easier access to all sorts of materials in recent centuries, styles are changing much more quickly today than they did thousands of years ago. New styles often respond to or oppose previous designs, but new buildings can also take inspiration from older styles.

The styles we will show you in this chapter don't come close to covering the many styles all over the world, but we'll take a look at a few that have been influential and widespread.

VERNACULAR ARCHITECTURE

Regional vernacular architectural styles exist around the world. They are formed naturally by people and communities living close to each other. Communities form relationships with nearby groups of people, and over time, they end up sharing customs and traditions, including food, music, clothing, language, and building styles. Vernacular styles form naturally, out of necessity—so a farming village in Idaho is very different from a village in Kenya or adobe dwellings in New Mexico. These styles develop based on people living their lives; for example, the people use local materials to build structures, and they eat food that is readily available or easy to grow in their area. These cultures often don't have specialists like contractors and architects. Families build their homes together based on information and knowledge that is passed down through the community over time.

ADOBE DWELLINGS FOUND IN SOUTHWESTERN UNITED STATES

BUILD A LOG HOUSE

Imagine you're in a pine forest region and you need to build a house. Show how you would build it using materials you can easily find nearby, with the help of the tools listed below. Draw a step-by-step diagram to explain your process.

Here are the tools available to you:

- Horse
- Cart pulled by the horse
- Wheelbarrow

- Saw big enough to cut down a tree
- Hammer and nails

- Ax
- Glass panes
- Flowing river nearby

CLASSICAL ARCHITECTURE

Classical architecture refers to ancient Greek and Roman designs from more than 2,000 years ago. This style encourages very grand and proud-looking buildings, and use of **pediments** and the **classical orders** is common. Classical buildings often sit high on **plinths** and have grand steps to show religious or civic importance—an example is the Parthenon in Athens, Greece. In Roman classical architecture, you see a lot of arches, **arcades**, and domes. Classical architects pay a lot of attention to form, proportions, and light.

Unlike vernacular building styles, which usually remain close to their places of origin, classical architecture significantly influenced many civilizations around the world. You can still see elements of it today, even on the simplest of homes, libraries, shops, and courthouses, especially in Western cultures. Many common elements of classical architecture are often made of strong materials such as stone, which lasts for a long time. This is one reason classical architecture has sustained its influence for so long.

ARCADE: side-by-side arches

ATLANTES: columns shaped like a man

CARYATIDS: columns shaped like a woman

CLASSICAL ORDERS: the form and decoration types of Greek and Roman columns—Doric, Ionic, and Corinthian

PEDIMENT: the triangular upper part of the front of a building in classical style

PLINTH: an architectural base for a column, sculpture, or building

PORTICO: a porch-like outdoor roofed structure held up by columns and usually attached to a building

CLASSICAL ARCHITECTURE

RAISING THE ROOF

In classical architecture, **caryatids** and **atlantes** act like columns, but they are shaped like humans!

Draw a collection of buildings whose roofs are held up by sculptures of your friends, classmates, or family members. You could also go a step further and, instead of drawing people, draw objects that represent those people. I might draw a porch being held up by stacks of books because my mother likes to read a lot. Or I might use kitchen tongs or a frying pan for my father, because cooking is his passion.

LATIN AMERICAN ARCHITECTURE

Central and South American Indigenous civilizations are all distinct, but they have many stylistic similarities. The Aztecs (Mexico) and Incas (Peru) flourished between 600 and 700 years ago; the Olmecs and Mayan civilizations (Mesoamerica) are much older, from about 1200 to 400 BCE. All these cultures had religious beliefs that were literally carved into all aspects of their architectural designs. Hallmarks of their structures are their bright colors, open spaces, patterning, and texture. Buildings and spaces were frequently oriented and arranged together in villages or city-states surrounding iconic stepped pyramids.

Although the architectural styles of these civilizations were largely uprooted by European colonialists, many of the stylistic elements have stood the test of time through other means. You can see evidence of their aesthetics in modern tapestries and pottery, as well as through bright colors and open courtyards in modern Latin American architecture. Some architects choose to gain inspiration directly from these older civilizations. For example, Frank Lloyd Wright paid tribute to Mayan architecture in several of his buildings.

A MAYAN TEMPLE

RUBBER BALL AND CHOCOLATE PARK

The Olmec civilization is credited with inventing the rubber ball and chocolate. It is only fitting that you design a park and arena where people can go to watch and play a variety of rubber-ball sports and games. You can line the walkways with concession stands built specifically for selling chocolate ice cream on hot days and hot chocolate on cool nights. A thrilling game of kickball followed by ice cream—what could be better? Make a list of what your park will include, then draw your design here.

Chocolate things in park

* _____

* _____

* _____

Rubber-ball things in park

* _____

* _____

* _____

FENG SHUI

Feng shui (pronounced "fung shway" and translated as "wind-water") is an ancient Chinese system of design that promotes harmony and balance between people and places. It is called a "system" instead of a "style" because the focus is more on how a space feels than how it looks. Feng shui design responds to qi (pronounced "chee"), which refers to energy that flows through the natural environment and our bodies. In this system, it is important to consider how a building and its occupants interact with the landscape's existing flow of energy.

Because it is a system, feng shui can be incorporated into any type of building. Because it isn't dependent on specific forms, it has different kinds of rules than most architectural styles do. Feng shui responds to each site individually. For example, if a wall facing a hill feels too large and rigid, an architect or occupant might choose to simply cut a hole in it, angle it, or slope it. This allows light, air, and other energies to pass through, by, or over the wall.

APARTMENT WITH FENG SHUI

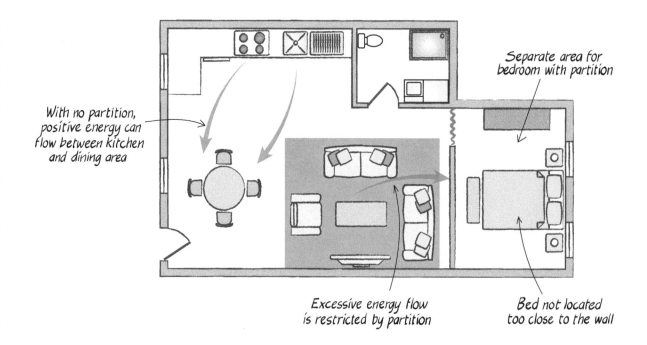

With no partition, positive energy can flow between kitchen and dining area

Separate area for bedroom with partition

Excessive energy flow is restricted by partition

Bed not located too close to the wall

BEDROOM FLOW

Feng shui principles are often applied to how furnishings are arranged. Draw a floor plan of your bedroom and show everything as it is right now, including clothes, shoes, and towels on the floor—whatever you see. Ask yourself questions about what is easy or frustrating about how things are arranged.

- Can you see who's coming into your room while you're in bed?
- Is your bed in a corner?
- Are corners dark or cluttered?

Sketch out a redesign of the room for ideal visual and physical flow.

VASTU SHASTRA

Vastu Shastra, which translates as "the science or study of architecture," is a design system from ancient India. As with feng shui, the focus is on promoting human well-being rather than dictating how buildings look. Vastu Shastra places importance on orientation and alignment with Earth's cardinal directions: north, south, east, and west. In this system, the square is considered the most ideal shape. Vastu Shastra also encourages open centers, such as courtyards, for fresh light and air and to help with energy flow.

People who practice Vastu Shastra believe this system balances the positive energies of five basic natural elements: sun, moon, wind, magnetic poles, and fire. They believe that without this balance, they will experience agitation, sadness, poor health, and economic decline.

ANGKOR WAT IN CAMBODIA

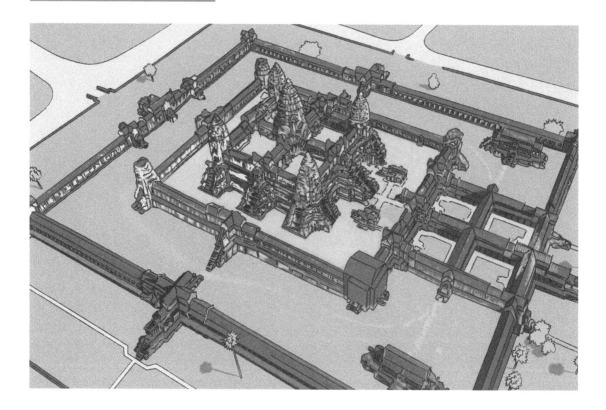

VASTU SHASTRA HOUSE

Grab a piece of paper and design a courtyard house using the principles of Vastu Shastra. Make sure you use the diagram as a design guide.

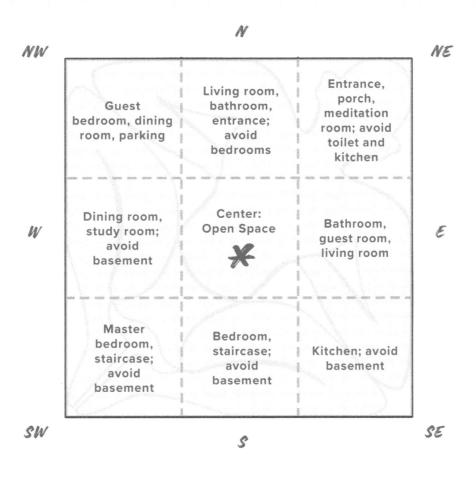

ISLAMIC ARCHITECTURE

Islamic architectural style is easily recognized in buildings across the world, but it is most common in the Middle East, Indonesia, and northern parts of Africa and India, where Islamic communities are prevalent. Although this style mostly evolved and spread with the religion of Islam, elements of Islamic architecture are not found only on religious structures.

Islamic places of worship, called mosques, often have tall decorative towers called minarets. The minarets have speakers that call local Muslims to prayer five times a day. Mosques, and other elaborate buildings of this style, often have horseshoe-shaped domes, multifoil arches, and intricate geometric wall carvings called arabesques. Their patterns usually include overlapping and intertwined circular and square forms that repeat over and over across an entire surface. Interior decorations often include very shiny tiles and mirrors that glisten in the light. In religious contexts, these geometric patterns represent the idea of a perfect divine creation, and the repetition symbolizes the infinity of the heavens above.

MOSQUE WITH MINARETS

NEIGHBORHOOD WITH A MOSQUE

You are given a plan oblique drawing of an urban neighborhood with bare buildings, streets, and sidewalks. Design a mosque with a courtyard and minaret in Islamic style in the empty lot. Then fill out the other building facades with related characteristics. Add lively activities, such as people dining or shopping on the sidewalk. Also add trees, streetlights, cars, and street furniture (such as benches, mailboxes, and traffic signs).

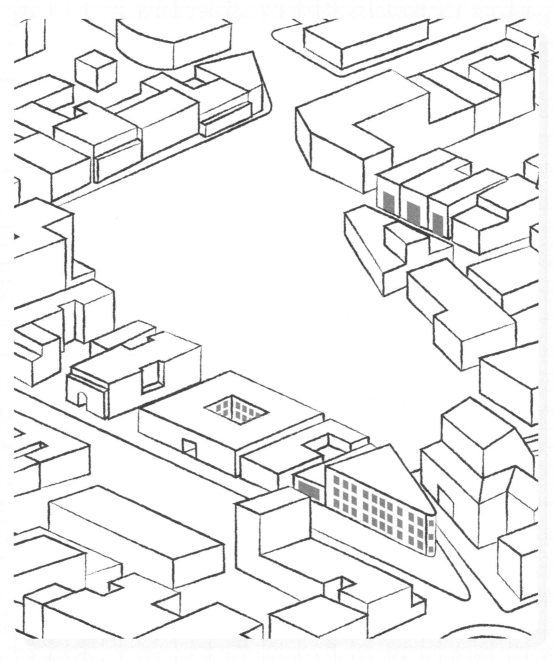

INTERNATIONAL STYLE

International Style became popular in the early 20th century, when architects from Europe and the United States responded to the conditions they were experiencing: the dirt and grime of the industrial revolution, overcrowded cities, and the aftermath of World War I. These architects wanted to create clean buildings with no frills—just simple, angular, machine-like forms. They used a lot of steel, glass, and concrete to make their minimalistic structures. They didn't add any extra decoration, either; they let the building parts and connections between them be the artistic expression. Architects of this style were the first to use glass to make walls. This helps inhabitants connect to the healing qualities of nature while still being safe inside a building.

This new kind of architecture is often called *modern architecture*, but when it caught the attention of the world, it quickly became a truly international style. You can see its influence today in cities across the globe.

INTERNATIONAL-STYLE HOUSE

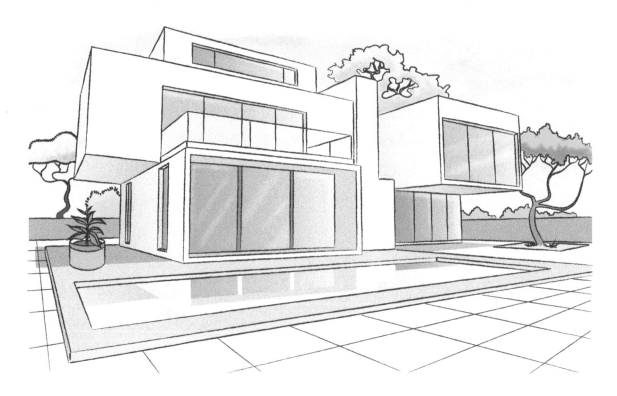

LIVING IN A GLASS HOUSE

Ludwig Mies van der Rohe and Philip Johnson are both architects who were active in the 20th century. They are famous for designing steel and glass houses in private garden settings. Design a steel-framed house whose outside walls are floor-to-ceiling glass. You can install curtains where privacy is essential, but design it so that its openness to the landscape and the outside environment celebrates nature. Would it be nice to feel almost like you're outside when you're indoors? What would your bedroom look like?

GOTHIC ARCHITECTURE

Each new style of architecture comes with bold and sometimes shocking experiments for its time. For Gothic architecture, this seems like an understatement. When this style emerged in the 12th century, it was awe-inspiring and dramatic. Gothic architecture was born out of Christian inspirations to make churches and cathedrals taller, brighter, and more colorful. Pointed arches and towers physically and symbolically reach higher to the heavens. Flying **buttresses** brace taller, thinner walls to help them stand up to the heavy weight of the building. Taller windows brighten and color cathedrals' interiors with natural light and stained glass. Gargoyles animate buildings with life and intrigue while also redirecting rainwater off rooftops.

Styles have influences far beyond their creators' intentions. Gothic architecture actually inspired a spinoff style on college campus buildings called *Collegiate Gothic*. Gothic style has also inspired whole genres of mystery and fantasy stories, movies, and games.

BUTTRESSES: Building elements such as roofs, domes, and arches can create outward and sideways pressure on the walls below. A buttress is a structural feature that acts against this pressure, called *lateral forces*. Buttresses are often seen on tall churches and cathedrals, and they can be very decorative.

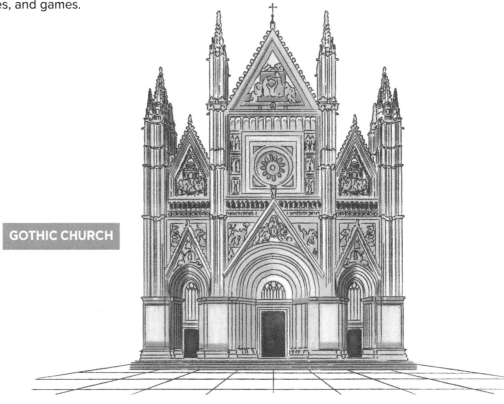

GOTHIC CHURCH

GOTHIC ARENA

Design a sports arena in Gothic style. Think about what a sports arena needs to have: lots of seating, a field or court, food vendors, staircases and ramps, and bathrooms. How can elements and principles of Gothic architecture enhance these structures? Consider function and how the arena looks from both the inside and the outside.

Sketching tip: A section drawing is probably the best way to see how your stadium functions. It helps you see how the seating and balconies relate to the field.

Super Cool Structures

EIFFEL TOWER: The 1,000-foot Eiffel Tower served as the entrance to the 1889 world's fair and to commemorate Bastille Day in celebration of the birth of the French Republic 100 years earlier. At the time, it was the tallest structure in the world. It still towers over Paris because of the strict height limits for most of the buildings in the city's historic center. The same architecture firm also designed and constructed the Statue of Liberty for the United States.

GREAT PYRAMID OF GIZA: This is the oldest and largest of the three pyramids in Giza, Egypt. Its construction began around 2580 BCE. It was the world's tallest human-made structure for about 4,000 years, until the Eiffel Tower came along. The pyramid was a massive undertaking of human ingenuity and an incredible physical accomplishment. Historians and architects still don't know exactly how it was constructed. It is believed that it was built as a tomb for the Egyptian pharaoh Khufu and took 20 years to build.

EIFFEL TOWER

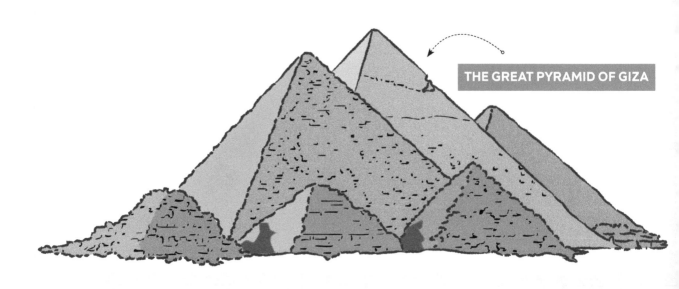

THE GREAT PYRAMID OF GIZA

CHRYSLER BUILDING: This building in New York City is one of the best-known high-rises in the world. It was the world's tallest building when it was completed in 1930, but within a year, it was surpassed by the Empire State Building. It has a kind of modern glamour, with its art deco style. This style, with geometric and automobile-inspired patterns, was requested by the founder of the Chrysler Corporation, which commissioned this building.

SYDNEY OPERA HOUSE: Designed by Jørn Utzon, this building is daring and iconic. Completed in 1973, the Sydney Opera House belonged to a later wave of modern buildings famous for molding and shaping concrete into curved shapes rather than straight rectangular forms. The shell-like forms that accentuate the surrounding water have become a recognizable symbol of Sydney and Australia.

SYDNEY OPERA HOUSE

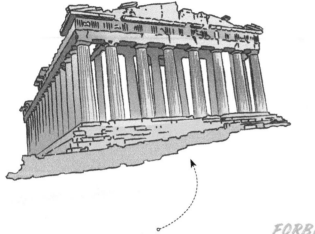

PARTHENON

PARTHENON: This marble temple built in the 5th century BCE was designed and constructed with no straight edges! It was built as a pagan temple dedicated to Athena, the goddess of wisdom, arts, literature, and war. A 40-foot statue of Athena once stood inside the temple. It is no longer there, but you can find a smaller replica of Athena in Nashville, Tennessee.

FORBIDDEN CITY: This is the world's largest imperial palace complex and was home to 24 Chinese emperors over 600 years. It's called the Forbidden City because only the emperor, his family, and his officials were allowed inside. It consists of almost 1,000 buildings surrounded by a high wall and a moat. It was designed in the traditional Chinese architecture style, and its medieval wooden structures have been carefully preserved.

FORBIDDEN CITY

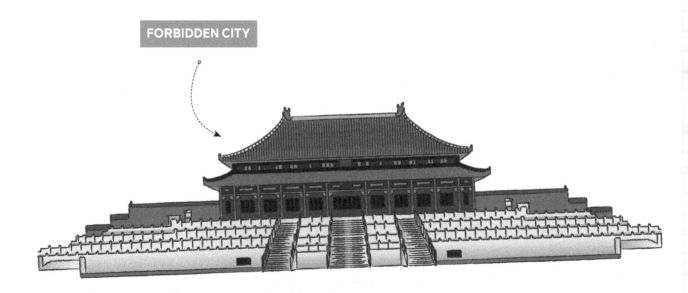

LEANING TOWER OF PISA: This marble bell tower in Pisa, Italy, was built on soft ground, causing it to lean to one side. It was started in 1173, but it took 177 years to complete because construction was halted so many times due to the sinking foundation. For more than 800 years, it slowly continued to lean more and more until engineers and architects in the 1990s worked together to protect it from leaning further. It is so famous for its construction flaw that engineers decided not to try to straighten it fully. The tower's lean is part of its identity now and expresses a fascinating history.

TAJ MAHAL: This structure in India was built in the 1600s as a mausoleum (a building that contains a tomb) for the Mughal emperor's beloved wife. The famous building, recognized by its large, pointed dome surrounded by four smaller domes, is the mausoleum, which is actually part of a larger complex that includes a garden, a mosque, and other buildings. The mausoleum is made of bright white marble and has detailed designs created with semiprecious stones. No later additions or alterations were allowed to be made to the Taj Mahal.

TAJ MAHAL

CHAPTER CHALLENGE

Do you have a favorite building or structure in your town or city, or maybe in a place you visited? What do you love about it? What do you know about it? (For example, when was it built and why?) Amazing structures don't have to be really old or in a faraway place. Maybe your favorite doesn't even exist yet and is a Super Cool Structure of the future! Aspiring architects will read about it years from now. Imagine this structure as a travel poster, a postcard, or part of an architecture photobook, and sketch it out.

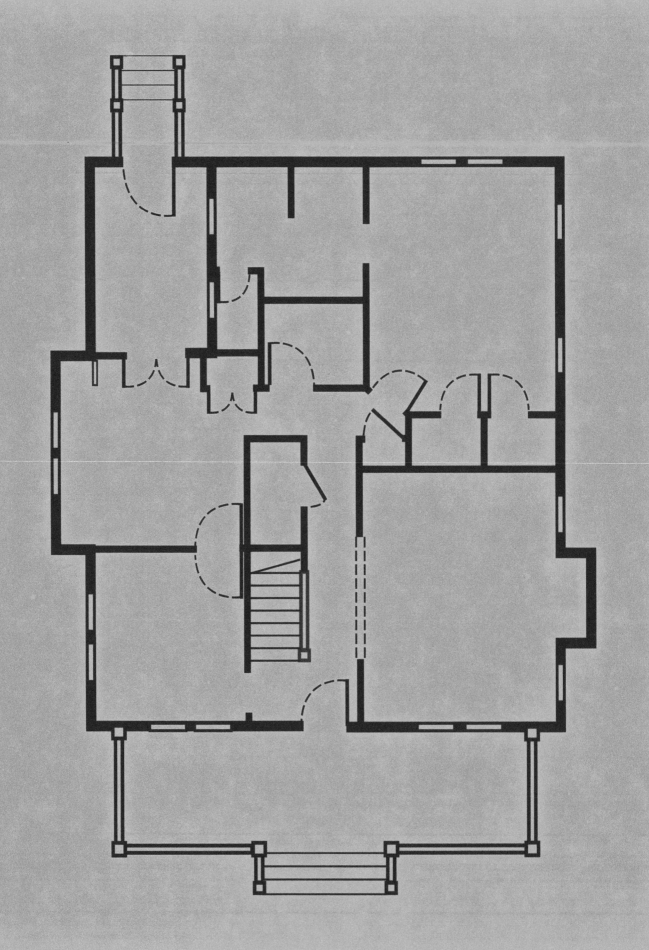

PART II

Design Your Dreams

We hope you liked learning all about architecture and what architects do. Now you'll have the chance to put some of those skills and concepts you learned to the test!

PLANTING A ROOF

Have you ever seen a green roof or visited a rooftop garden? Just as their names imply, they are rooftops covered with grasses and other ground-cover plants. The plants help handle the runoff from snow and rain. A green roof doesn't have to be completely filled with plants; it can also be occupied by people. Design a green rooftop here with a furnished area under the pergola where people can relax and enjoy the views. What kinds of plants and flowers would be ideal?

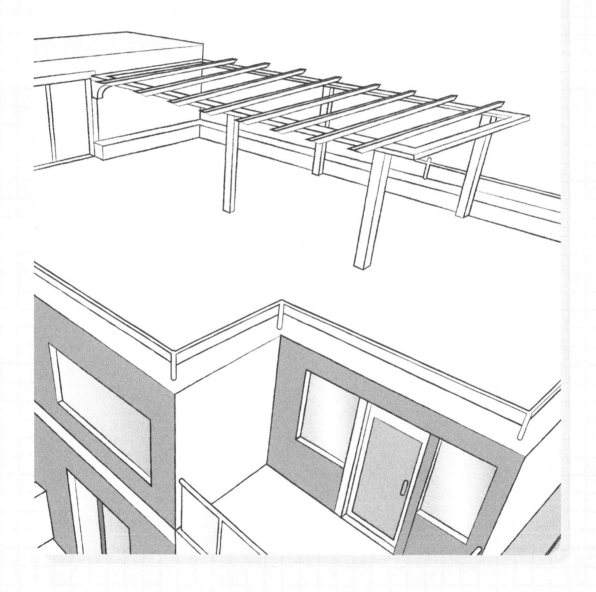

MY BUILDING BFF

Create a building inspired by your best friend. Make a list of their personality traits and one activity or hobby of theirs that makes them special. Then design a space that reflects their identity and helps them do an even better job on their hobby.

_____'s personality traits:

1. _____   3. _____

2. _____   4. _____

_____'s hobby/activity:_____

_____'s space:

MUSEUM OF ARCHITECTURE

Imagine you're a famous architect, and you've been asked to curate (select and put together) a museum exhibit featuring some of your favorite buildings. Come up with a creative name for the exhibit and a short summary to excite visitors, then sketch out a drawing of how the exhibit would look. Think about your favorite architectural styles.

Name of exhibit: _____

Summary of exhibit: _____

_____

_____

Design of exhibit:

EUROPEAN VACATION HOME

You've been asked by a Finnish couple, one a painter and one a sculptor, to design a vacation home with two smaller guest dwellings, a courtyard, and a shared art studio. The couple wants the structures to fit into and mimic the surrounding hilly landscape. The **design precedent** they want you to follow is Säynätsalo Town Hall in Finland (see illustration). They like the brick, the sharp angles, and the flow of the courtyard space to the street.

> **DESIGN PRECEDENT:** an existing construction, architectural project, or art piece that serves as inspiration for a design project. Architects do not copy precedents; they borrow ideas from them.

SÄYNÄTSALO TOWN HALL

TINY HOUSE CHALLENGE

Tiny houses are becoming popular with people who want to live simply in a small space without a lot of stuff. Most tiny houses are small enough to be hitched to a pickup truck and driven to a new location! Your client has asked you to design a tiny house that is 324 square feet: the size of a large living room. How will you arrange it to include a bed, sitting area, kitchen, bathroom, and storage, all in that space? How about a washing machine? (Tip: A tiny house can be up to 13½ feet high.) Use your imagination! Would you like to live in a tiny house?

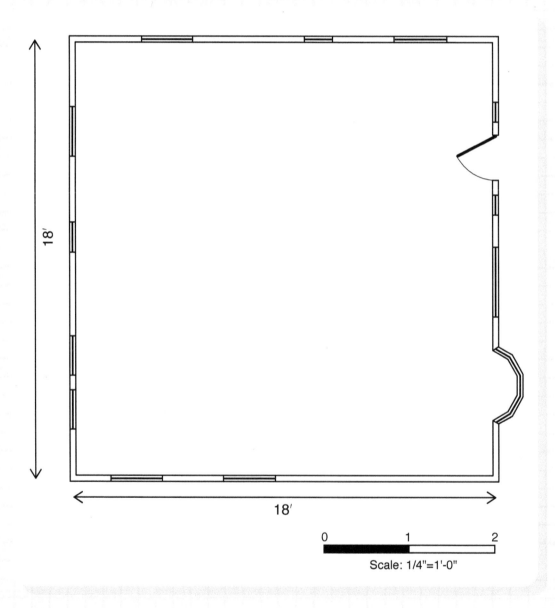

18'

18'

0   1   2

Scale: 1/4"=1'-0"

BUILDING BODY LANGUAGE

Body language can tell people if you are happy, mad, proud, or sad. What does a building's "body language" say to the world?

Draw three buildings that represent three emotions of your choosing. Think about how materials affect the mood. Does wood siding feel different from concrete blocks or red brick? Consider the placement of windows and doors. How does it affect the attitude if you make the windows really high? What about if you make them crooked? Also think about the overall shape of the building. Is it tall or short? Pointy or rounded?

Building #1

Mood: _____

Building #2

Mood: _____

Building #3

Mood: _____

NOTRE DAME'S ROOF

After the roof of the Notre Dame Cathedral in Paris burned in 2019, people all over the world wondered whether the old roof would be replicated or if a totally different roof would be built. Design a proposal for an entirely new roof for Notre Dame.

DESIGNER CLOTHING

What if the zigzag patterns of stepped pyramids influenced the zigzag patterning in tapestries and clothing in Latin countries? Decorate an outfit inspired by your favorite architectural style that you learned about in chapter 4.

Favorite architecture style:_____

Outfit pattern:

TRY TESSELLATION

Tessellation is a pattern that intertwines shapes so that no space in a surface is left undesigned. Create your own tessellation, and fill the space on this page with your designs.

   Example steps: 1. Start with a lightly drawn square. 2. Change the left side to a new shape. 3. Trace it and replace the right side with the same shape. 3. Do the same thing with different shapes at the top, and copy it to the bottom.

   Do you see what's happening? You're making a tessellation that can be copied—infinitely! In the sample, you can insert other shapes, like a circle. Draw your tessellations right next to each other so they create a pattern.

HOW TO MAKE TESSELLATIONS

HELLO, HIGH-RISE

In 1871, there came a surge of buildings with a vertical (height) and commercial emphasis. The world had never seen this building type: the high-rise. Made mostly with steel or iron frames, these buildings reached to the sky and provided nearly limitless views.

Architects debated what style they should be: classical, **neoclassical**, Gothic, or something else. In the following pages, create high-rise elevation drawings. Borrow from the styles mentioned in this book, do your own research, or pull from your imagination!

For each elevation, draw two floor plans—one for the street level and one for a higher floor. The building can be for anything: offices, apartments, a business, or anything else you can come up with.

NEOCLASSICAL: Meaning "new classical," this term refers to 18th- and 19th-century buildings designed to look like classical styles of ancient civilizations.

CONTINUED >

UNDER THE SEA

You're designing a house that's part of an underwater community, but you can only use locally sourced materials. What would you use to create the floor? Seashells? Driftwood? Maybe an area rug made out of woven seaweed? What about the roof, door, and windows? Brainstorm your materials, then draw out your design here.

Roof:_____   Walls:_____

_____   _____

Doors:_____   Furniture:_____

_____   _____

Windows:_____   _____

_____   _____

DRAWING DOWNTOWN

In the next two pages, draw a **street plan** of a city's downtown area. Let the street flow from one page to the next. Include street intersections and **pocket parks** every once in a while. Make the buildings different sizes and shapes, and include sidewalks, trees, parking and bike lanes. On the two pages after that, draw a facade for each of the buildings you drew in the street plan. Think about different architectural styles you learned about, and consider what a downtown area needs—stores, restaurants, and so on. Get creative! Add fun things such as roof gardens, cool sculptures, or your dream candy store.

> **STREET PLAN:** a bird's-eye-view drawing of a street, to include rooftops
>
> **POCKET PARK:** a small urban park at a street corner or tucked between buildings

CONTINUED >

SNACK SHACK

Design a house made of snack foods such as crackers, nuts, and pretzels. Draw a facade elevation here. Label your materials. Think about sizes, shapes, firmness, and softness. What might be strong enough for a column? What's a good idea for roof shingles? Brainstorm your snack ideas before you start sketching (try not to get too hungry!).

Roof:_____

Windows:_____

_____

_____

Foundation:_____

Walls:_____

_____

_____

Doors:_____

Furniture:_____

_____

_____

CREATE A QUESTIONNAIRE

A post-occupancy evaluation (or P.O.E.) helps architects see how successful a building is after people have been living or working in it for a certain period of time. Develop a P.O.E. questionnaire about the living room in your house for your family members to fill out. Ask them questions that will help you see how the design is working, how it could be better, and how important the issues are to them. We have added a few questions to help you get started!

How many years have you been using this living room? _____

How many hours per day do you spend in the living room? _____

What is your favorite part of the living room? Why?_____

KID'S KITCHEN

Design a kitchen based on your needs as a kid. Kitchens can be intimidating, uncomfortable, and not approachable to younger people! They can have flames and sharp knives and tall cabinets out of reach. What would your ideal kitchen be like? Think about size and scale, safety, sunlight from windows and what you want and need from your kitchen. Draw your ideas here.

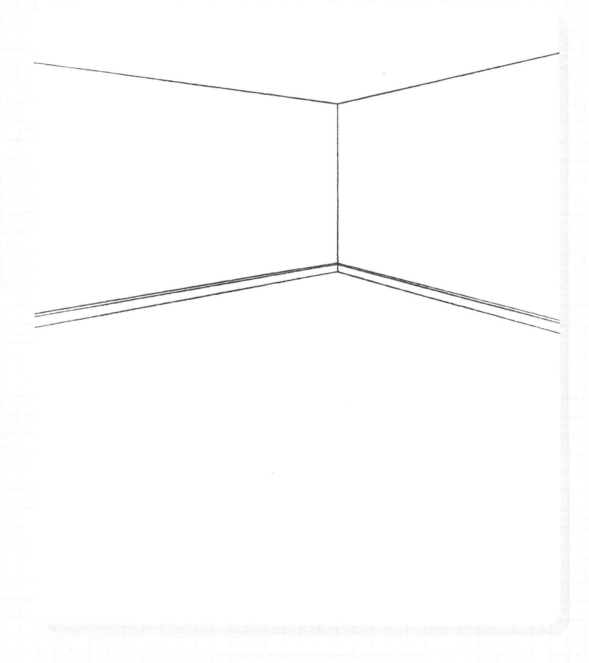

WHAT'S THE WORD?

Close your eyes, open a dictionary to a random page, and point to a word with your finger. Write the word in the space here. Use that word to inspire a design for a store logo.

Word: _____

Type of store: _____

Logo:

POP!

Pop architecture refers to structures whose design is based on common items or household objects. Pick an object from your bedroom—a toy, a book, a clock, a game, whatever you like—and design a pop architecture structure inspired by that.

TEXTURES AND PATTERNS

In the squares provided, do rubbings and pattern drawings of different textured surfaces in your home, such as brick, tile, carpet, or concrete. To do a rubbing, lay this page on top of a textured surface and gently color in one square. To make a pattern drawing, find a patterned material that wouldn't show up in a rubbing, like a smooth ceramic tile or a striped rug. Then draw the pattern in one of these squares. Be sure to label the patterns and include color!

DOOR-TO-DOOR

Take a walk around your neighborhood or do a Google image search to explore different kinds of doors. Look for swinging doors, sliding doors, roll-up garage doors, and any others you can find. Look for similarities, differences, decorations, and other unique characteristics. In the space provided here, draw some of the ones that grabbed your attention. Then pick your favorite and design a welcome mat for it!

Doors:

Welcome mat:

MAKE AN ENTRANCE

One way that architecture involves choice is through different options to move between spaces. Use the basic floor plan—imagine each room has different heights—and decide what each room is for and then design how to access each area. Would inhabitants need stairs? An elevator? Maybe a slide? A ramp? How does the transportation tie into the purpose of each room?

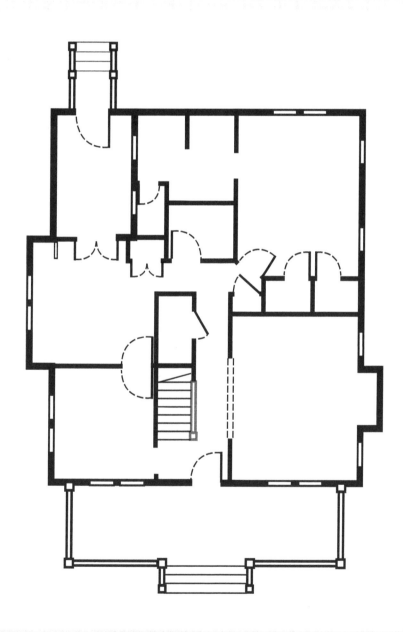

MY TOWN SQUARE

The architect Léon Krier said that a town should be kind of like a pizza. (No, he didn't mean piping hot and covered with cheese!) He meant that, like each slice still has all the ingredients of the whole pizza, each neighborhood should have all the ingredients of a full city. A neighborhood should be complete enough that its inhabitants don't have to travel far to get groceries, hang out at a park, or go to school.

Your job is to design a neighborhood around a public square. Your town square should have everything its inhabitants need for daily living, including houses or apartments, a library, restaurants, places of entertainment, a hair salon, and so on.

You have a lot of space for this activity, so use it! Create a bird's-eye-view drawing of your neighborhood to show how buildings and nature interact. Then draw five elevations, sections, or floor plans for your favorite individual buildings. Make sure you include natural elements, such as trees, gardens, and people.

Bird's-eye view of neighborhood:

Five buildings in my neighborhood:

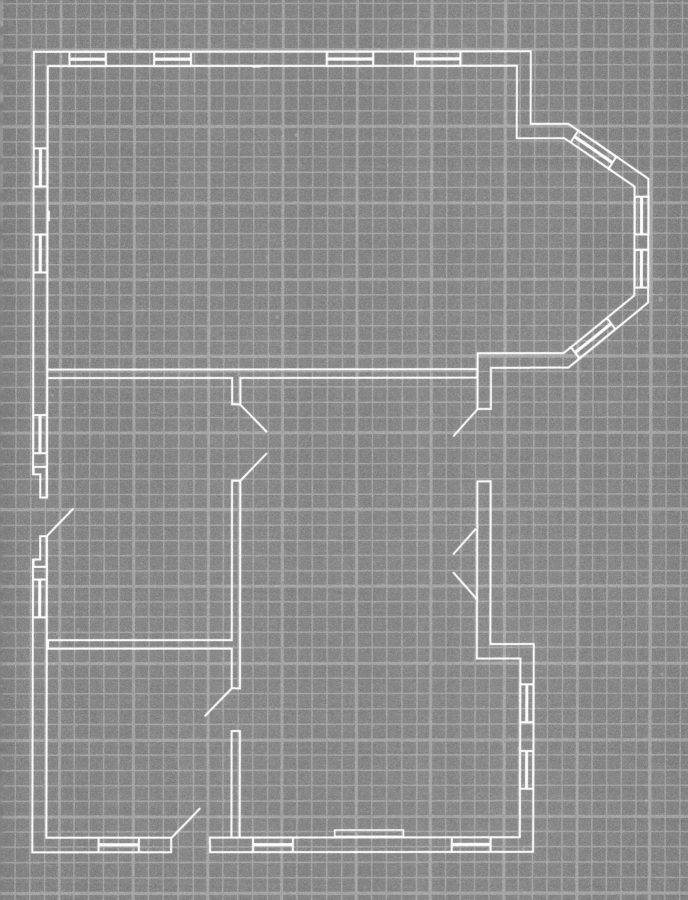

Resources

Web Pages and Videos

Renaissance Kids Architecture Camp and the Household Edition: Founded and directed by this book's author, Mark Moreno
Andrews.edu/renkids

NOMA: National Organization for Minority Architects: Project Pipeline
NOMA.net/project-pipeline

Learn about the golden rectangle:
youtu.be/c8ccsE_lumM

Learn about drawing types, elevations, plans, and sections, drawn on glass:
youtu.be/pzKHy5RFBao

Draw a tree with a swing (by the author):
youtu.be/xBTWVP8EtxY

"One Skill (+ item) Every Aspiring Architect Needs"
youtu.be/YYW7exK_ml8

Books and Additional Websites

- The author sometimes read to his college students *If You Give a Moose a Muffin*. It's such a wonderful reflection of how ideas flow from one to another in the design world.

- Many ideas about urbanism come from Jane Jacobs's book *The Death and Life of Great American Cities*.

- The Congress for the New Urbanism (CNU.org) is a wonderful resource for understanding how architecture and urbanism are beautifully interdependent.

- In his book *Léon Krier: Houses, Palaces, Cities*, Krier likens a city to a pizza: the parts need to be layered rather than experienced one at a time.

- Project for Public Spaces (PPS.org) is a great resource for helping people make local places better.

Acknowledgments

Mentors outside of one's immediate family are a treasure. Mine are Mr. Pete Hernandez, Ms. Artie Mae Carter, Mr. John G. Cocharo, Mr. Dick Powell, and Professor John Maruszczak. Thank you to all Renaissance Kids and their parents for their continued interest and support. Many thanks to all of the fantastic camp assistants throughout the years, but especially this year's team, whose participation directly helped this book: Darius Bridges, Dorcas Hakiza, Emony Wood, Isaac Wood, Jenalee Holst, and Maryza Eguiluz. Special thanks to Mr. Praful Shintre for his friendship, general support, and insightful discussions about Vastu Shastra. And special thanks to my colleague Professor Tom Lowing for counterbalancing my right brain.

About the Authors

Mark Moreno is an associate professor of architecture at Andrews University's School of Architecture and Interior Design. He is 59 years old, and when he grows up, he wants to be curious.

Professor Moreno has architecture degrees from Harvard University and the University of Texas at Arlington. He has taught at four universities, worked in a handful of offices, and lectures about creativity and hands-on education. His academic scholarship focuses on several areas: placemaking, person-environment relationships, and kitchen and bath design. In 2011, he received the Daniel A. Augsburger Excellence in Teaching Award at Andrews.

He shares his expertise widely within his community to promote walkability, accessibility, and quality sense of place. His creative scholarship and deep passion for children's education are manifest in the Renaissance Kids Architecture Camp and the new online version called the "Household Edition." Since 2007, when Professor Moreno founded the program, more than 1,000 children ages 5 to 16 have participated in creative, hands-on learning experiences and collaborative community-based build projects, such as sitting spaces, playhouses, doghouses, and lemonade stands. Without Renaissance Kids, this book would not be possible.

Siena Moreno is Mark's daughter, and she inherited his love and passion for the arts, working with children, hands-on creations, and classic rock. She earned her bachelor's degree in art theory and practice and English literature from Northwestern University in 2018, and she is currently pursuing a master's degree in school counseling. Siena lives in Arizona and works at a high school helping students graduate and pursue postsecondary education.

Siena has no idea what she wants to be when she grows up, but she is confident that she will always be working with children and teens. She hopes to never stop pursuing her passions and wants to encourage others to do the same. Siena loves sunshine, dark chocolate, blueberries, and sass.

Printed in the USA
CPSIA information can be obtained
at www.ICGtesting.com
JSHW071742031023
49387JS00004B/16